The wonder of sisters

C.R.Gibson®
FINE GIFTS SINCE 1870

All images © Hulton Getty Picture Collection
Design by Keith Jackson
All text unless otherwise attributed by David and Rebecca Pickering.

Developed by Matthew A. Price, Nashville, Tennessee.

Published by C. R. Gibson®
C. R. Gibson® is a registered trademark of Thomas Nelson, Inc.
Nashville, Tennessee 37214
Printed and bound by L. Rex Printing Company Limited, China

ISBN 0-7667-6160-6
UPC 082272-44981-7
GB4137

the wonder of sisters

"For there is no **friend** like a **sister** In **calm** or **stormy** weather; ..."

"...To **cheer**
one
on the
tedious
way ..."

"...To fetch one if one goes astray..."

"...to lift one
if one
totters
down, ..."

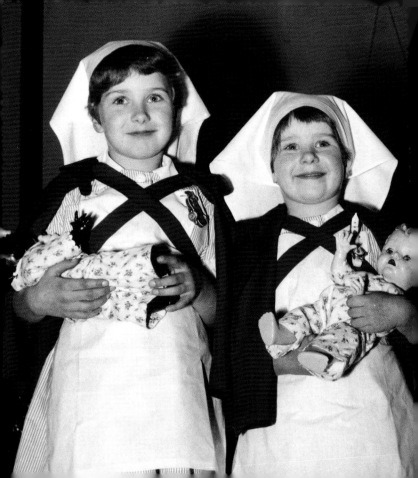

"...To strengthen whilst one stands "

– Christina Rossetti

"sisters
start
life very
small..."

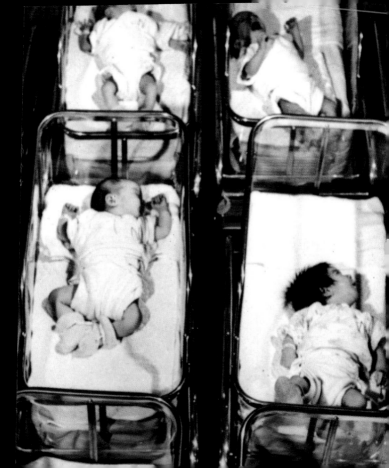

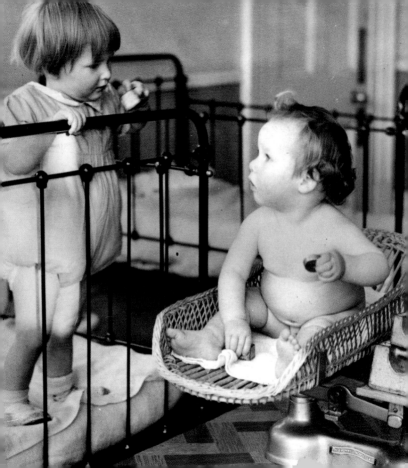

"...and even
when they're
only little
they start to be
your
friend"

"They keep you **company** – they're **always** there for you"

"Sisters are
practical..."

"...and have a
sense
of style"

"Sisters
are there to
play with
you..."

"They share their
lives with you"

"Sisters **know** you **inside** and **out...**"

"...but love you in spite of the little flaws they see"

"No **touch** is more **wonderful** than a sister's **hand**"

"Friends come and go but sisters are forever"